Sharks

by Amelia Penn

W
FRANKLIN WATTS
LONDON • SYDNEY

First published in 2012 by
Franklin Watts
338 Euston Road
London
NW1 3BH

Franklin Watts Australia
Level 17/207 Kent Street
Sydney
NSW 2000

Picture credits: Shutterstock: cover, 8, 13, 21; istockphoto: 4-5, 6-7, 18, 19; Nature PL: 9, 11, 15, 16-17; David Fleetham/ Visuals Unlimited Inc/Getty Images: 12. Every attempt has been made to clear copyright. Should there be any inadvertent omission please apply to the publisher for rectification.

A CIP catalogue record for this book is available from the British Library.

Dewey number: 597.3-dc23

ISBN 978 1 4451 0321 1 (hbk)
ISBN 978 1 4451 0329 7 (pbk)

Series Editor: Melanie Palmer
Series Advisor: Catherine Glavina
Series Designer: Peter Scoulding

Printed in China

Franklin Watts is a division of Hachette Children's Books, an Hachette UK company. www.hachette.co.uk

Contents

Words in **bold** can be found in the glossary.

What is a shark?

A shark is a type of fish.
There are over 350 kinds,
in all shapes and sizes!

The whale shark is the biggest fish in the world.

Shark skeleton

Sharks don't have bones. Their bodies are made of a material called **cartilage**.

Cartilage is light, so it is easy for sharks to swim fast.

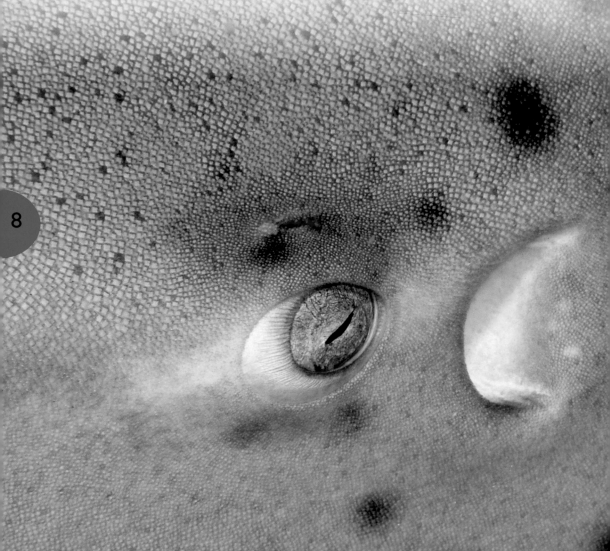

Shark skin

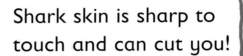

Shark skin is sharp to touch and can cut you!

Shark skin is made of thorny **scales**, like sharp teeth. They are called **denticles**.

Shark senses

Sharks can feel movement far away. This makes them good at **hunting** food!

Some sharks hunt seals. They smell them before they see them.

shark teeth

Sharks that hunt have many rows of strong, pointed teeth.

If a tooth falls out, another one takes its place!

Safe sharks

The biggest sharks
are also the safest.
Whale and Basking
sharks only eat tiny
living things
called **plankton**.

Shark spotting

The eyes on a Hammerhead shark are far apart, so they see things faster.

17

Some sharks are named after their shape, like the Hammerhead.

Dangerous sharks

Great White sharks can be dangerous, but they do not attack people very often.

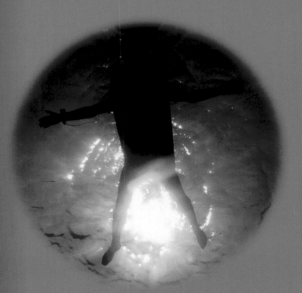

Surfers can look like tasty seals to a hungry shark.

Shark school

Many people study sharks to find out how they live. We can learn a lot about sharks.

What would you like to find out?

Glossary

Cartliage - light, bendy material

Denticles - sharp points on a shark's skin

Hunting - looking for animals to kill and eat

Plankton - tiny living things that float in water

Scales - thin covering of skin on fish

Senses - smell, sight, touch, taste and hearing

Websites:

http://www.kidszone.ws/sharks/facts.htm

http://kids.nationalgeographic.com/kids/animals

http://sharkfacts.org

Every effort has been made by the Publishers to ensure that the websites are suitable for children and that they contain no inappropriate or offensive material. However, because of the nature of the Internet, it is impossible to guarantee that the contents of these sites will not be altered. We strongly advise that Internet access is supervised by a responsible adult.

Quiz

1. Which shark is the biggest fish in the world?

2. What do Basking sharks eat?

3. What is a shark's body made of?

4. Which shark is called after its funny-shaped head?

5. What happens when a shark's tooth falls out?

6. Even if a shark can't see you, how may it know you are near?

The answers are on page 24

Answers

1. The Whale shark
2. Plankton
3. Cartilage
4. Hammerhead
5. A new tooth takes its place
6. It can smell you or feel you move!

Index